This Book Belongs To ...

....

....

....

....

Date _____ *adress:* _____

Name : _____

School: _____

Year old: _____

When I started playing basketball : _____

Now I play at : _____

My coach is : _____

Why I like my coach: _____

_____

_____

My coach often tells me: _____

_____

_____

_____

Why I like playing basketball : _____

_____

_____

_____

My goal is : _____

_____

_____

_____

From Monday _____ to Friday _____ How many times _____
                Date   Date

1st practice was: Very easy ☐ Easy ☐ Average ☐ Hard ☐ Very hard ☐
2nd practice was: Very easy ☐ Easy ☐ Average ☐ Hard ☐ Very hard ☐
3rd practice was: Very easy ☐ Easy ☐ Average ☐ Hard ☐ Very hard ☐

1st practice: 🙂 😐 🙁   2nd practice: 🙂 😐 🙁   3rd practice: 🙂 😐 🙁

Coach focused on
_____
_____
_____

I focused on
_____
_____

What I'v learnt
_____
_____

My weaknesses/strengths
_____
_____

Coach advice
_____
_____

Additional notes
_____
_____

Date_____/_____/_____ Page No:

My Picture And Note

My Picture And Note

_____

_____

_____

_____

_____

_____

_____

Date_____/_____/_____   Page No:

Date_____/_____/_____   Page No:

My Picture And Note

_____

_____

_____

_____

_____

_____

_____

Date: _____ / _____ / _____   Page No:

My Picture And Note

Date_____ / _____ / _____   Page No:

My Picture And Note

My Picture And Note

Date _____ / _____ / _____   Page No:

Date_____/_____/_____   Page No:

My Picture And Note

Date_____/_____/_____   Page No:

My Picture And Note

_____

_____

_____

_____

_____

_____

Date____/____/____   Page No:

My Picture And Note

Date_____/_____/_____   Page No:

My Picture And Note

Date _____/ _____/ _____   Page No:

Date_____/_____/_____   Page No:

Date_____/_____/_____   Page No:

My Picture And Note

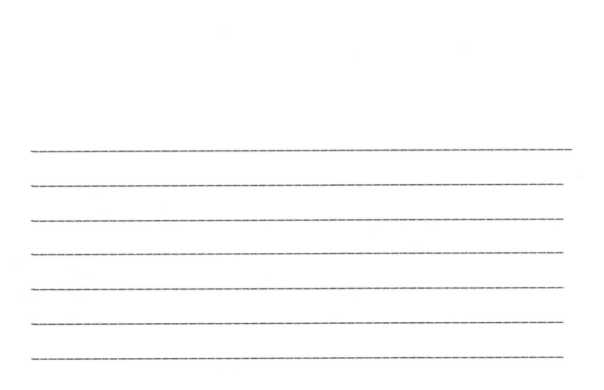

Date_____/_____/_____   Page No:

My Picture And Note

_____

_____

_____

_____

_____

_____

_____

My Picture And Note

My Picture And Note

_____

_____

_____

_____

_____

_____

_____

Date_____/_____/_____   Page No:

Date_____/_____/_____   Page No:

My Picture And Note

Date ___/___/___ Page No:

My Picture And Note

Date_____/_____/_____ Page No:

My Picture And Note

My Picture And Note

Date_____/_____/_____   Page No:

My Picture And Note

My Picture And Note

Made in the USA
Monee, IL
21 November 2021

82682904R00059